SHARK FRENZY

Whale Sharks

by Rebecca Pettiford

BELLWETHER MEDIA • MINNEAPOLIS, MN

Blastoff! Readers are carefully developed by literacy experts to build reading stamina and move students toward fluency by combining standards-based content with developmentally appropriate text.

Level 1 provides the most support through repetition of high-frequency words, light text, predictable sentence patterns, and strong visual support.

Level 2 offers early readers a bit more challenge through varied sentences, increased text load, and text-supportive special features.

Level 3 advances early-fluent readers toward fluency through increased text load, less reliance on photos, advancing concepts, longer sentences, and more complex special features.

★ **Blastoff! Universe**

Reading Level

Grade
K

Grades
1-3

Grade
4

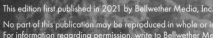

This edition first published in 2021 by Bellwether Media, Inc.

No part of this publication may be reproduced in whole or in part without written permission of the publisher. For information regarding permission, write to Bellwether Media, Inc., Attention: Permissions Department, 6012 Blue Circle Drive, Minnetonka, MN 55343.

Library of Congress Cataloging-in-Publication Data

Names: Pettiford, Rebecca, author.
Title: Whale sharks / by Rebecca Pettiford.
Description: Minneapolis : Bellwether Media, [2021] | Series: Blastoff! Readers: Shark frenzy | Includes bibliographical references and index. | Audience: Ages 5-8 | Audience: Grades 2-3 | Summary: "Simple text and full-color photography introduce beginning readers to whale sharks. Developed by literacy experts for students in kindergarten through third grade"-Provided by publisher.
Identifiers: LCCN 2020001603 (print) | LCCN 2020001604 (ebook) | ISBN 9781644872505 (library binding) | ISBN 9781681037134 (ebook)
Subjects: LCSH: Whale shark–Juvenile literature.
Classification: LCC QL638.95.R4 P48 2021 (print) | LCC QL638.95.R4 (ebook) | DDC 597.3/4–dc23
LC record available at https://lccn.loc.gov/2020001603
LC ebook record available at https://lccn.loc.gov/2020001604

Editor: Rebecca Sabelko   Designer: Kathleen Petelinsek

Printed in the United States of America, North Mankato, MN.

Table of Contents

What Are Whale Sharks?

Whale sharks are the largest fish on Earth. They can grow as big as a school bus!

These slow giants live in oceans all over the world. They are found in coastal areas, but they also swim in the open ocean.

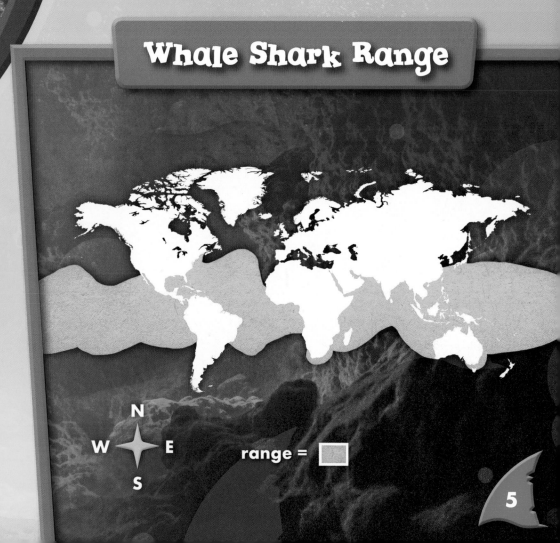

Whale Shark Range

range =

N
W   E
S

5

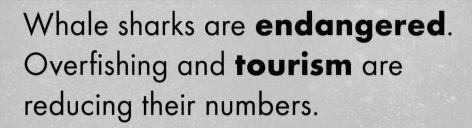

Whale sharks are **endangered**. Overfishing and **tourism** are reducing their numbers.

scientist studying
a whale shark

Even with efforts to save them, their numbers continue to fall. But scientists are trying to find ways to help them.

Spotted Giants

Whale sharks are gray,
blue, and brown.
Their bellies are white.

White spots and stripes cover their backs and sides. Every whale shark has its own pattern.

snout

Whale sharks have wide,
flat heads and round **snouts**.
Their large mouths are at the
front of their snouts.

Their mouths open about 5 feet (1.5 meters) wide!

Shark Sizes

average human   whale shark

6 feet (2 meters) long • - - - - - 🤿

up to 66 feet
(20 meters) long

Hungry for Plankton

Whale sharks have 3,000 tiny teeth! They are set in 300 rows.

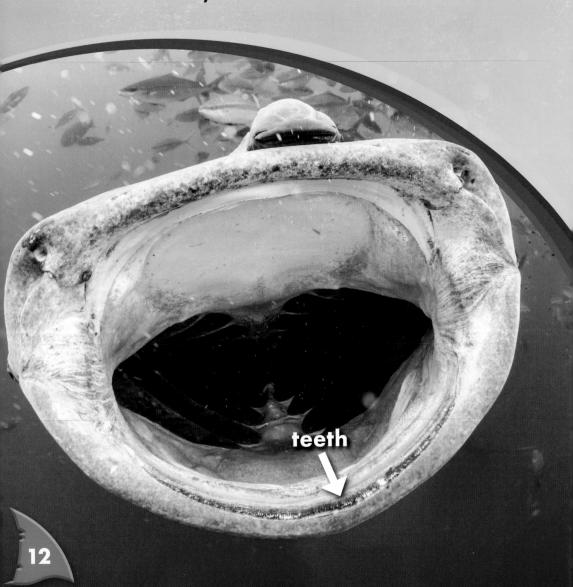

teeth

Identify a Whale Shark

white spots
and stripes

round
snout

gills

But these sharks do not use
their teeth to eat. They eat
prey in a different way!

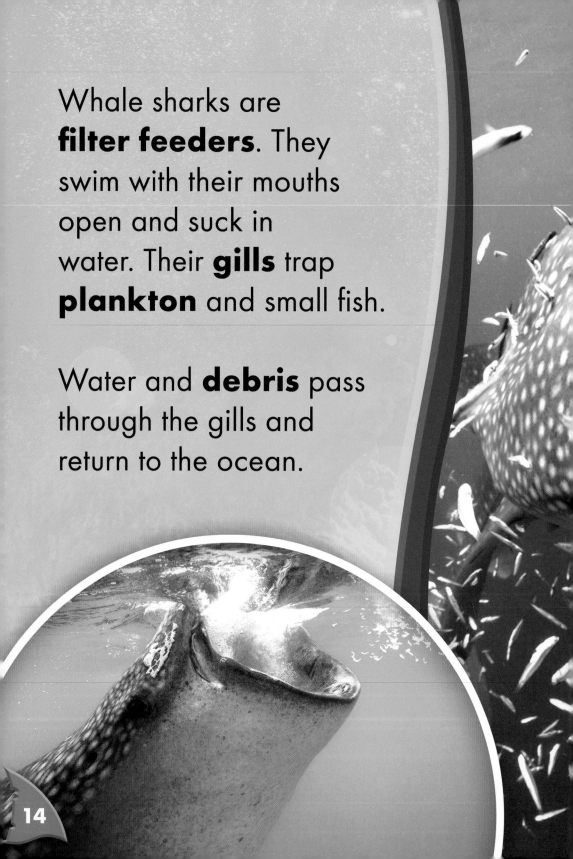

Whale sharks are **filter feeders**. They swim with their mouths open and suck in water. Their **gills** trap **plankton** and small fish.

Water and **debris** pass through the gills and return to the ocean.

Whale sharks need to eat a lot of food! They often eat shrimp and squids. They also love fish eggs.

Some **migrate** across oceans to find **spawning** fish and **plankton blooms**.

Whale Shark Diet

plankton

shrimp

small fish

17

Whale sharks do not have **predators** because they are so big.

Whale sharks are not a danger to humans. They are gentle giants of the sea!

Deep Dive on the Whale Shark

LIFE SPAN:
up to 150 years

LENGTH:
up to 66 feet (20 meters) long

WEIGHT:
up to 40,000 pounds
(18,144 kilograms)

DEPTH RANGE:
more than 2,297 feet
(700 meters)

white spots
and stripes

round snout

gills

Least Concern	Near Threatened	Vulnerable	Endangered	Critically Endangered	Extinct in the Wild	Extinct

conservation status: endangered

Glossary

debris—pieces of waste or remains

endangered—animals or plants that are in danger of dying out

filter feeders—ocean animals that take in many small pieces of prey at one time

gills—parts that help sharks breathe underwater

migrate—to move from one area to another, often with the seasons

plankton—ocean plants or animals that drift in water; most plankton are tiny.

plankton blooms—large numbers of plankton in one area

predators—animals that hunt other animals for food

prey—animals that are hunted by other animals for food

snouts—the noses of some animals

spawning—relating to fish that are releasing eggs

tourism—the activity or business of traveling to a place for fun

To Learn More

AT THE LIBRARY

Gleisner, Jenna Lee. *Whale Shark*. Minneapolis, Minn.: Jump!, 2020.

Shea, Therese M. *Whale Shark: The Largest Fish*. New York, N.Y.: PowerKids Press, 2020.

Tunby, Benjamin. *Whale Sharks in Action*. Minneapolis, Minn.: Lerner Publications, 2018.

ON THE WEB

FACTSURFER

Factsurfer.com gives you a safe, fun way to find more information.

1. Go to www.factsurfer.com.

2. Enter "whale sharks" into the search box and click 🔍.

3. Select your book cover to see a list of related content.

Index

The images in this book are reproduced through the courtesy of: Krzysztof Odziomek, front cover; Andrea Izzotti, pp. 3, 13; wildestanimal, p. 6; Simon Pierce/ Alamy, pp. 6-7; Leith Holtzman, pp. 8-9; Fata Morgana by Andrew Marriott, pp. 10-11; petesphotography, pp. 12-13; Frolova_Elena, p. 14 (inset); Reinhard Dirscherl/ Alamy, pp. 14-15; Rich Carey, pp. 16-17; Choksawatdikorn, p. 17 (plankton); Mati Nitibhon, p. 17 (shrimp); Mr. JK, p. 17 (small fish); Onusa Putapitak, p. 18; orifec_a31, pp. 18-19; WhitcombeRD, pp. 20-21, 21 (gills).